Battles of the Civil War

Wendy Conklin, M.A.

Table of Contents

The War Between the States

The Civil War dragged on for four long, bloody years. It was the most destructive war in United States history. More Americans died in this war than in any other war. Some battles raged in cities and others near the **plantations** (plan-TAY-shuhnz) in the South.

The North fought to save the Union. The South fought for the right to **dissolve** (dih-ZALV) the Union. In the end, the Union stayed together, but the battles left wounds that took years to heal.

▼ The ruins of Richmond, Virginia, after the Civil War

How the War Began

The Civil War was under way long before any soldiers fired their guns. The battle grew in people's hearts and minds. Politicians (pol-uh-TISH-uhnz) in the North wanted to end slavery. The Northerners had built factories and did not use slaves. In the Declaration of Independence, it says, "all men are created equal." Some Northerners wanted to uphold these words.

Robert E. Lee decided to fight for the South because of his love for Virginia.

Who Fought the War?

The Civil War was fought between the North and the South. Soldiers in the South were called **Confederates** or rebels. Northerners were called Yankees or **Union** soldiers.

Many people in the South believed the Northerners were threatening their way of life. The southern plantations supplied most of the region's money. If there were no slaves, who would do the work on the plantations? How could the South survive with no money?

The South believed they had a right to break away from the Union. The breakup of the Union began in 1860. This is when South Carolina **seceded** (suh-SEED-ed) from the United States of America.

Expanding Slavery

Many Southerners not only wanted to keep slavery in their states, but they also wanted the new western states to allow slavery.

▼ The country during the Civil War years.

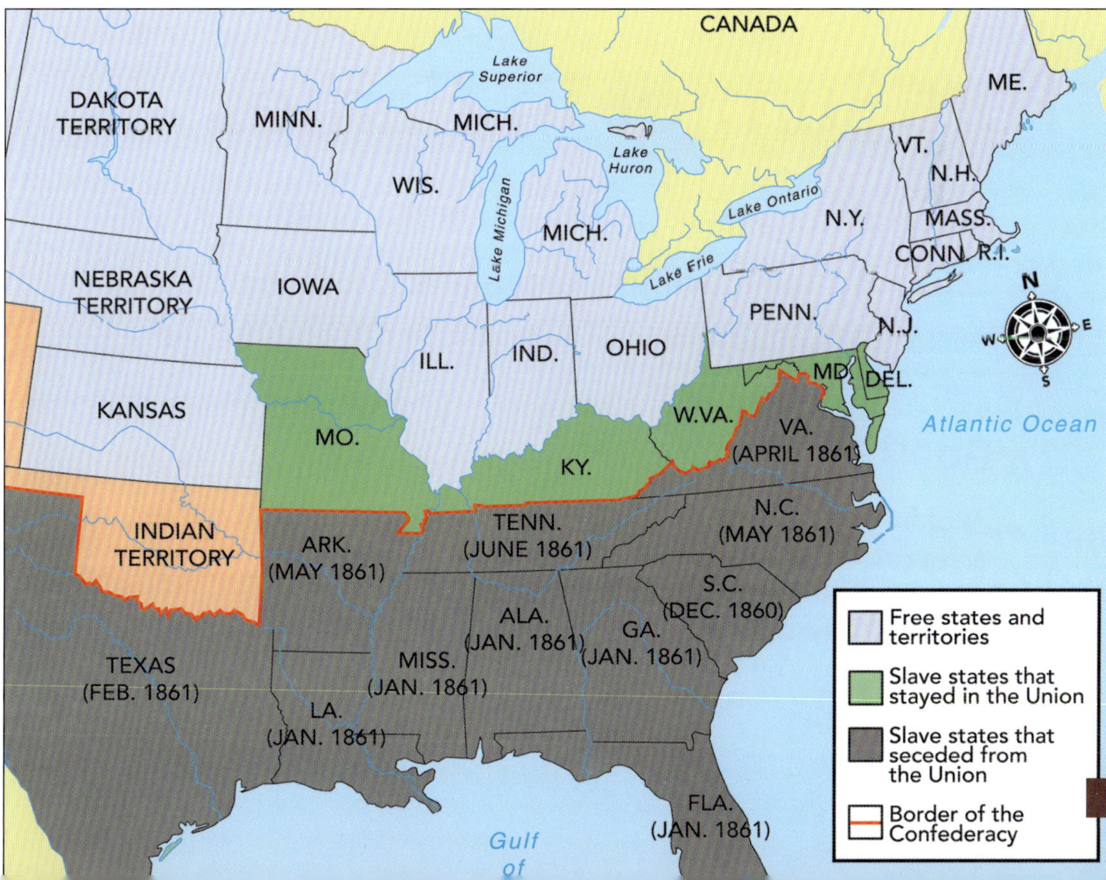

▲ The bombing of Fort Sumter near Charleston, South Carolina

Fort Sumter in Flames

Fort Sumter sat on an island off the coast of South Carolina. By 1861, South Carolina had left the Union. In spite of this, Union soldiers stayed at that fort. The Confederates (kuhn-FED-uhr-uhtz) did not like this at all.

When the soldiers at the fort ran low on food, President Abraham Lincoln sent a supply boat to the men. He told South Carolina's governor that the boat would not

A Good Show

Thousands of Southerners saw the battle at Fort Sumter. They loaded their carriages up with food and friends. Then, they watched as the bombing took place near Charleston.

have any guns or soldiers. The Confederates refused to allow this or any other boats near the fort. In fact, they demanded that the fort **surrender** (suh-REN-duhr).

Robert Anderson, the commander at the fort, said, "We will not surrender!" He and his 68 men braced for an attack. On April 12, 1861, Confederate General P.G.T. Beauregard (BOH-ruh-gahrd) ordered his troops to fire cannons at the fort. Fort Sumter went up in flames and Anderson surrendered after two days. This was the true beginning of the Civil War.

No Casualties

Despite heavy firing, not one man died during the attack on Fort Sumter.

▼ Fort Sumter after the bombing

The Battle of Bull Run

In July 1861, many of the rich men and women from Washington, D.C., came to see the next big battle. They sat on a hillside to watch. The location of this battle was Bull Run, a small creek in northern Virginia.

General Irvin McDowell was in command of 34,000 Union men. But the Union men were not trained soldiers. They did not know how to fight and sometimes even ignored orders.

Newspapers and politicians had been pressuring President Lincoln to end the war. In return, Lincoln pressured General McDowell to attack the Southerners. McDowell knew his men were not ready, but he obeyed the president's orders to attack.

The Legend of Stonewall Jackson

General Jackson held his rebel troops on top of Henry House Hill. They stood firm and stopped the northern attack. Through the smoke, a southern soldier cried out, "There is Jackson standing like a stone wall!" After the battle, Jackson was called "Stonewall Jackson" by soldiers in the North and South.

General Thomas "Stonewall" Jackson

▲ **Intense fighting at the Battle of Bull Run**

At first, it looked like the Union forces would win the Battle of Bull Run. They drove the southern army back and over a hill. But, Confederate General Thomas Jackson's men held their position. They sent the Union soldiers running back down the hill.

The Union attacked again, but Jackson's men stood firm along the crest of the hill. A high-pitched scream broke out along the Confederate line. It was the first (but not the last) time the Union forces heard the spine-chilling "Rebel Yell." With that, the rebels ran down the hill charging at their enemy. Panic spread and the Union men ran for their lives.

Bloody Shiloh

In 1862, the Confederate leaders created a plan to take control of Tennessee. They decided to attack the Union forces under General Ulysses S. Grant. The northern soldiers were camping near Shiloh, Tennessee, and did not suspect anything.

At dawn on April 6, 1862, some Union men were eating their breakfasts when they heard a rebel yell. Union General William Sherman saw rebels streaming in from the woods. He rallied his men to stand firm. Sherman's men fought fiercely. Other northern soldiers ran away from the fight.

General Grant raced to the battle from a few miles away. He found soldiers running away from the fight. He turned them around, and they fought the Southerners all day long. At nightfall, Confederate General Beauregard called off the battle and claimed a victory for the South.

The Battle of Shiloh in Tennessee was one of the bloodiest days of the war.

The next morning, Grant ordered a **counterattack** (KOUNT-uhr-uh-tak). The Northerners attacked across the fields where bodies lay from the day before. That afternoon Beauregard and the Confederates **retreated**. More than 23,000 Americans were dead.

Lincoln Defends Grant

The Northerners were angry with Grant for not being ready for the attack. They felt he should have prevented all the deaths. Lincoln defended him by saying, "I can't spare this man. He fights." Lincoln was frustrated with his other leaders who were backing down from big battles.

The Second Battle of Bull Run, August 29, 1862

The Battle of Bull Run, Again

In the summer of 1862, Confederate General Robert E. Lee took a huge risk. He knew that Union General George McClellan hoped to join up with General John Pope. Lee decided to attack Pope before McClellan's men had a chance to join them. Lee divided his army and sent one half to fight Pope and the other half to find McClellan.

General Jackson was among the leaders sent to attack Pope's men. Jackson ordered his men to go north and cut off the railroad supply to Pope. Jackson's soldiers made their way to the old Bull Run battlefield. While there, they found Union supplies. Jackson's men took some of the supplies and then burned all that remained.

Jackson's Foot Cavalry

Jackson marched his men so fast that they were soon called foot **cavalry** (KAV-uhl-ree). This joke meant that Jackson's men were as fast as horses.

When the two armies finally met, a huge battle began. After several attacks, the rebels withdrew to stronger **defensive** (duh-FEN-siv) positions. Pope thought they had retreated. He was surprised the next day when the Confederates put up another good fight. In the end, the Union soldiers retreated to Washington, D.C.

This alarmed people in the Union. The southern army was very close to the capital city. They feared that Lee's army would take over their capital. However, at that time, Lee did not have the strength to defeat the defenses around Washington.

Switching Jobs

After this key battle, President Lincoln made some changes. General McClellan replaced Pope as the commander of the Union army.

▼ This is a photograph of a bridge built during the Second Battle of Bull Run.

Invading the Union at Antietam

By late 1862, General Lee decided it was time to take the war to the North. The land and people in Virginia and other southern states had been run down by the war. Lee needed food and supplies for his men. So, Lee marched his army north into Maryland. Maryland's crops were plentiful and the shops were full of supplies.

This was the first time the armies were in the North. It would be very important to the Union army to stop Lee and his men. Then, a stroke of luck hit McClellan's army. A Union soldier found some cigars wrapped in paper. The paper had Lee's attack orders written on it. Historians think the cigars had fallen out of a Confederate officer's pocket.

Abraham Lincoln and Union officers after the Battle of Antietam

With this information, McClellan not only knew where Lee would be; he also knew what Lee was planning to do. The two large armies met near a small town on Antietam Creek.

Losing Many Good Men

In all, the lives of 23,582 families were affected at Antietam. A total of 3,620 men were killed in the one-day battle. About 17,365 soldiers from both sides were wounded. Another 2,597 men were missing or captured. This day is still considered the bloodiest day in American history.

The sides clashed on September 17, 1862. For 12 hours, they fought around a church, a sunken road, and a bridge. Several times, it seemed that General McClellan would win. But, he was not aggressive enough. He kept an extra 20,000 men in **reserve** instead of putting them into the battle.

Freeing the Slaves

Following the battle at Antietam, Abraham Lincoln made a very important announcement. Beginning on January 1, 1863, "all persons held as slaves within any State . . . in rebellion against the United States, shall be then, thenceforth, and forever free." This was called the Emancipation Proclamation. It was the first major step toward freeing the slaves in America.

Finally, night came and the battle ended. Lee's army was very badly hurt. McClellan should have launched a massive attack on the Southerners. However, McClellan failed to fight against Lee's battered army. Lee took his troops back to Virginia to get strong again.

Battling at Gettysburg

After Antietam, the southern army continued to win most of the battles. The North took huge **casualties** (KAZ-uhl-teez) at each battle. Within a year, Lee felt strong enough to move his army north again. This time, Lee's army advanced into Pennsylvania. Unfortunately for Lee, his **scouts** had not sent any information to him recently. He had no idea that he was about to run right into the Union army.

A huge battle began on July 1, 1863, in a small town called Gettysburg. As a small group of southern soldiers entered the town, northern cavalry shot at them. There were not very many northern soldiers in Gettysburg. However, the southern officers did not know that. So, they did not attack.

▼ This map of the battleground at Gettysburg was drawn just after the battle.

A general studies the battlefield.

Gettysburg Address

This three-day battle took the lives of more than 54,000 men. A cemetery was opened at the site of the battle to honor those men who died. President Lincoln was asked to say a few words at the **dedication** (ded-uh-KAY-shuhn) ceremony. His two-minute speech, the Gettysburg Address, is considered to be one of the most important speeches in history.

By the next morning, more soldiers for both sides had arrived on the battlefield. The Union soldiers dug in on Cemetery Hill, Culp's Hill, and the Round Tops. This high ground gave the Union soldiers an advantage. Lee ordered the rebels to charge up the hills and attack. By the end of the day, thousands of soldiers from both sides lay dead.

Lee's choices on July 3 are still questioned today. General Lee decided to attack the middle of the Union line. He hoped it would be the weakest point of the line. Lee sent General George Pickett's men across a mile of flat land. From the high ground, the Union army easily destroyed the attacking rebels. This single charge took 5,000 lives. Lee's army began its long retreat back to Virginia that night.

Siege at Vicksburg

Vicksburg, Mississippi, is located on hills that overlook the Mississippi River. This location was very important during the Civil War. The army that controlled Vicksburg controlled the great Mississippi.

Until 1863, rebel forces controlled the Mississippi River. There was no way to attack the city without facing Confederate soldiers. It was General Ulysses S. Grant's job to find a way into Vicksburg.

The Beginning of Grant's Power

General Grant was a general who was willing to lead fierce attacks against the enemy. Many of the other Union generals hesitated to attack. Lee's army was able to escape time and again when they should have been destroyed. President Lincoln needed a leader who would push the men and make them fight. Grant became the commander of the whole Union army in March 1864.

Grant sent his troops down the Mississippi River. He then had them march south of the city across the land. Over the next three weeks, Grant's men marched a great distance and won five battles. They then made their way to Vicksburg and attacked from the east. With no way to penetrate (PEN-uh-trait) the city, his forces dug in and waited. The Union forces blocked the city from receiving any outside supplies. This is called a siege (SEEJ).

Once the North controlled the Mississippi River, the Confederates could not use it to get supplies to their army.

As weeks passed, citizens of Vicksburg and the Confederate soldiers began to starve. Confederate General John Pemberton received a note on June 28. It read, "If you can't feed us, you had better surrender. Signed, Many Soldiers." On the night of July 3, the guns went silent and the rebels surrendered. This was a huge victory for Grant and his army.

Digging in Around Petersburg

After the Union victories at Gettysburg and Vicksburg, Northerners hoped the war would end quickly. Unfortunately, it was still almost two years before the fighting was done. There were a number of battles in early 1864. Then, starting in June 1864, the fighting centered around Petersburg, Virginia.

Petersburg was just south of the Confederate capital of Richmond, Virginia. The two armies faced each other from June 1864 to April 1865 near Petersburg. Grant dug trenches and laid siege to the city.

Grant did not think that he could break through the strong rebel lines at Petersburg. So, his men dug an underground tunnel that stretched all the way to the rebel lines. They filled

Soldiers in the trenches at Petersburg ▼

the tunnel with explosives and lit the fuse. The explosion created a large crater in the ground. Northern troops ran down into the crater hoping to run up the other side. The rebels fired into the crater and killed many Union soldiers. It was a terrible day for Grant and his men.

Grant lost two soldiers for every soldier that Lee lost. However, Grant had many more men in the North to serve as soldiers. So, the Union army remained strong.

The Crater Affair

General Grant said that the deaths at the crater were "the saddest affair I have witnessed in the war."

The fall of Petersburg

After the long siege, Lee finally had to move his men out of Petersburg on April 2, 1865. By leaving Petersburg, that meant Lee was also giving up the capital city of Richmond. Lee had no choice. His army was falling apart. He had to regroup if he was going to continue to fight.

Surrender at Last

Lee told his staff, "There is nothing left for me to do but go and see General Grant and I would rather die a thousand deaths." On April 9, 1865, Lee sent a note to General Grant. The two great generals rode to Appomattox (ap-uh-MAT-uhks) Court House, Virginia, to talk about the surrender.

Wilmer McLean owned a red brick house in the village of Appomattox Court House. It was at his house that Grant and Lee met. Lee arrived dressed in his best uniform with a sash and a sword at his side. Grant arrived directly from the field with mud-spattered pants and boots.

McLean's Luck

At the beginning of the war, Wilmer McLean owned a house near Bull Run Creek. The McLean family lived there during both the Bull Run battles. After his business failed, he moved to Appomattox Court House. It's funny that he moved away from the battlefields and still ended up having soldiers in his home.

Lee signing surrender papers

EXTRA.

Surrender of Lee

AND 30,000 MEN.

Peace in 6 Days

WASHINGTON, April 9, 10 P. M.

A dispatch from Secretary Stanton to Gen. Dix says:

A dispatch from Gen. Grant announces the surrender of Gen. Lee with 30,000 men.

Lee would not surrender to Sheridan, but rode furiously and successfully for an interview with Grant, to whom he surrendered, and was accorded the honors and privileges of a prisoner of war. Peace will undoubtedly be declared within six days.

Grant's Only Relief

General Grant had been suffering with a headache during the first days of April. When he received the note from Lee, his headache strangely vanished.

Grant wrote up generous terms of surrender. All he really asked was that the Confederate soldiers surrender their guns and return to their homes. The southern officers were allowed to keep both their guns and their horses. Grant also promised that the leaders would not be charged with **treason** (TREE-zuhn).

That night soldiers from both sides shared food. The war that had made friends fight against each other was finally over. Now, it was time for both sides to heal and to rebuild a united nation.

Glossary

casualties—soldiers who are killed or wounded in battle

cavalry—soldiers who ride horses in battle and are often scouts

Confederates—people who supported the South in the Civil War; comes from the name of the country formed by the states that seceded, the Confederate States of America

counterattack—to attack after having already defended a position

dedication—a ceremony to name or set aside somewhere for a special purpose

defensive—to protect against or prevent an attack

dissolve—to break apart

penetrate—to break through

plantations—large farms that produced crops for money

politicians—people who run for and serve in political offices

reserve—extra soldiers waiting to fight

retreated—pulled back or left a battle

scouts—soldiers who traveled in front of the main army to find out where the enemy was and to map the land

seceded—left or broke away from; states that left the Union

siege—a military blockade of an area that cuts off all contact with the outside world

surrender—to give up and lose a battle or the war

treason—when someone attempts to overthrow a government or does something that harms his or her country

Union—term used to describe the United States of America; also the name given to the northern army during the Civil War